for those who have fallen
under Angela's thrall

First published in 2013 by
SIDEKICK BOOKS

Reprinted in 2017

Typeset in Helvetica World
Title font: Lansbury
Sidekick Books logo font: Roman Antique

Extracts from the text were previously published in the p.o.w. broadside *Murder She Wrote* (2012)

www.sidekickbooks.com
http://chrissywilliams.blogspot.com
www.howardhardiman.com

~

ISBN: 978-1-909560-17-8

written by
CHRISSY WILLIAMS

illustrated by
HOWARD HARDIMAN

sidekickBOOKS
www.sidekickbooks.com

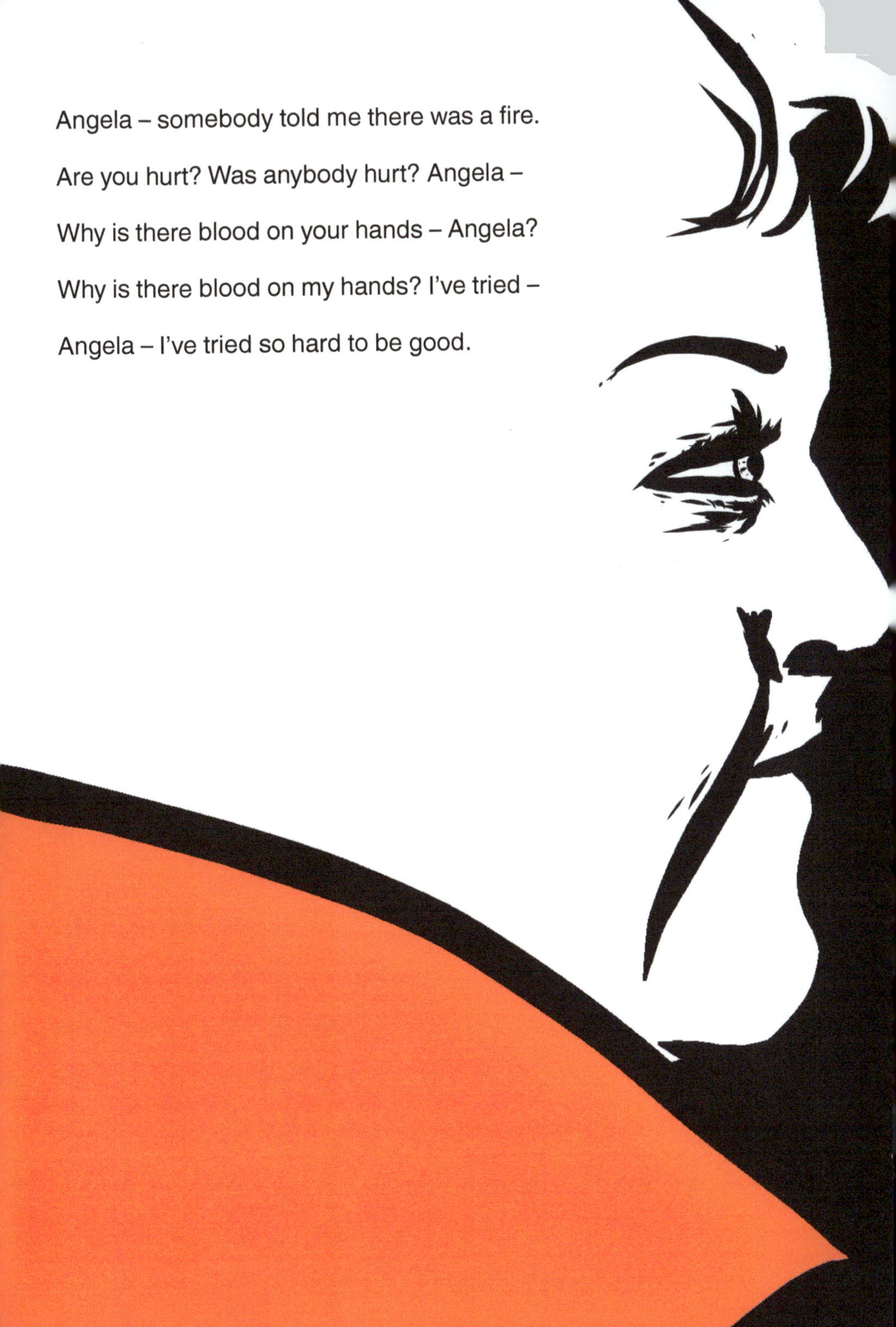

Angela – somebody told me there was a fire.

Are you hurt? Was anybody hurt? Angela –

Why is there blood on your hands – Angela?

Why is there blood on my hands? I've tried –

Angela – I've tried so hard to be good.

Angela – where is Jessica? Shouldn't she be here?
Her friends fall like leaves, the leaves, the leaves,
but she seems to hold on to her principles.
Angela – what do you mean "There is no Jessica"?

I don’t know what to do – Angela – what do you think?

Jessica wouldn’t lie. I don’t want to lie. But, okay –

Angela – let’s take some time. Forget the murder,

or lack of one. I want to talk about you.

Do you think this is our blood?

Do you know I think about you all the time?

Is that murder in your eyes? Could it be a wink?

Come along, Angela – don't corpse.

Angela – I've never met anyone like you – Angela.

You turn down ghosts and walk through blue gardens.

I will run through valleys to find you. Angela –

I keep a dagger in my bosom, buried deep.

Run with me through the graveyard – Angela –

We will pass the tiny Angela grave – Angela –

I'm trying to live free from devastation.

Spare me – Angela – run with me.

Angela – I've lost something – Angela –

but I don't know what it is. Perhaps

I am lost. Angela – You know what it is,

don't you? It's you – Angela – It's you.

In this blue garden, I cannot speak its name.

How did you make your way out of the story to find me?
Angela – not all plots are equal. You're amazing.
Please – Angela – please let me scream in whisper:
You're amazing. You're amazing. You're amazing.

I wish I had met you a thousand years ago – Angela.

You could have shown me things while I pointed out others.

Angela – every moment is lived simultaneously.

I am experiencing now all the mournful fruits of maturity.

But tell me – Angela – can't you taste them too?

Come closer – Angela – take a bite from my mouth,

from my heart.

Angela – it's not just me. I woke up this morning thinking about it happily. It's not just me. It's not just me. Oh Angela – the full horror is only just starting to sink in. It's not just me.

Confusion is the proper state of love.

Angela – you draw the dagger out,

keep drawing, keep on drawing.

This dagger never ends.

It pierces the heart. It pierces the eye.

It pierces more lives than we are able to bear.

Let’s hold hands in the cemetery – Angela –

where all the dead lie in their proper places.

There is to be no dramatic climax – Angela –
I wonder how your face would have looked,
frozen as the credits rolled over.
But there has been no death – Angela –
there's just us: two bungling murderers,
trying to avoid each others' eyes.

O – may your face

become a model of horror

to all who behold it.

O – may blood slip from your eyes

as softly as silk.

O – may your smile crack

to twice its beautiful width

and may all your tears fall

like skulls into empty graves.

Angela – I beg you. Stay.

I haven't thought about you for days – Angela –
I haven't thought about you for minutes.
I pass you on the shelf. I am ignoring you.
Watch me.

A kiss from you – Angela – would be catastrophic.

Angela – an extinction level event – Angela –

like kissing the face of destruction. Do not tempt me –

Angela – we both understand the violence of a kiss.

There is blood here – Angela.

I don't know whose blood it is.

I'm starting to think – Angela.

I'm starting to think.

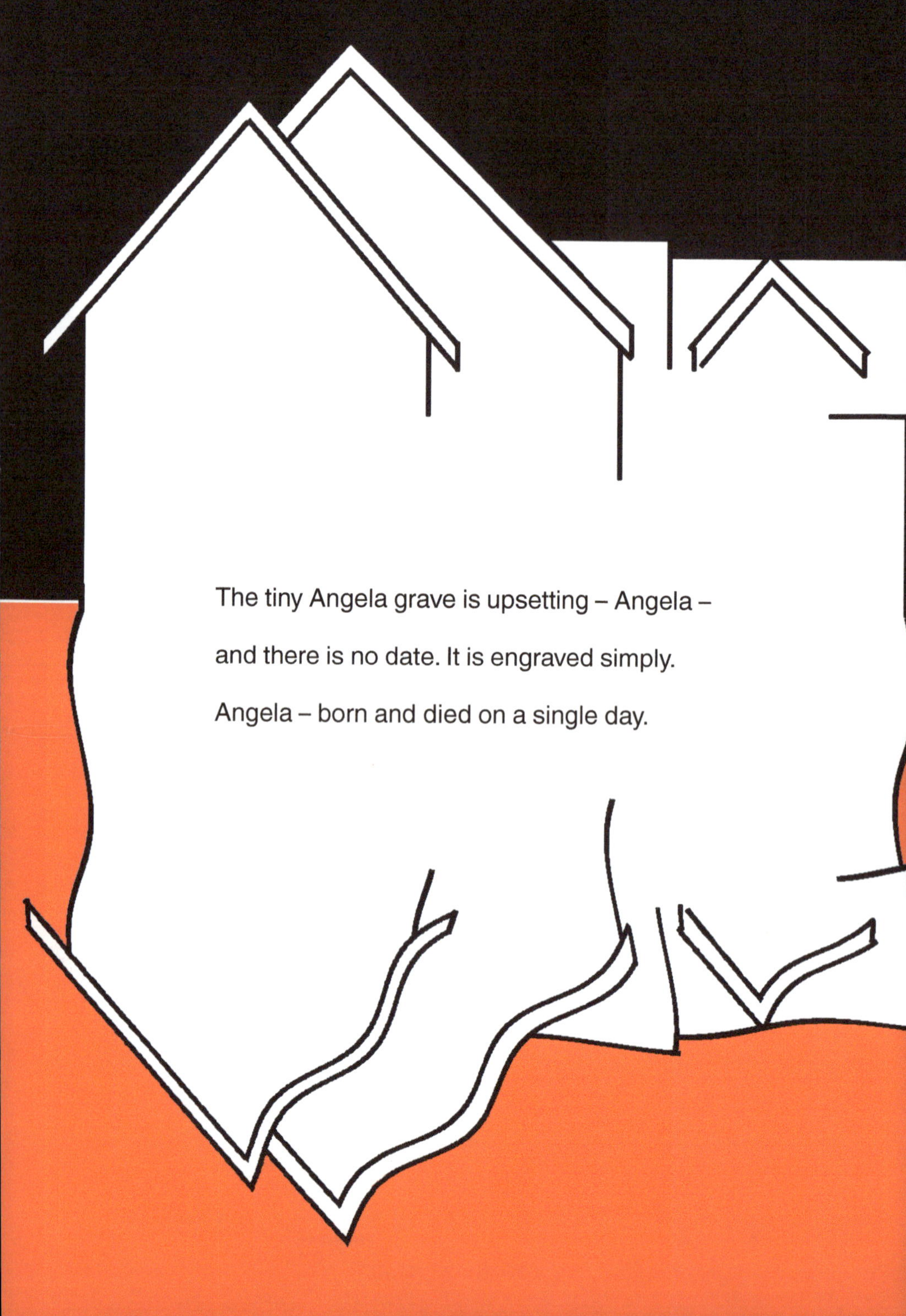

The tiny Angela grave is upsetting – Angela –

and there is no date. It is engraved simply.

Angela – born and died on a single day.

I need you – Angela – although I will never be in
your show – Angela – week after week – Angela –
you save the world, fight crime, oppose injustice.
I would not change your world for anything.
Angela – where there are no grey areas –
where nothing can be taken from you – Angela –
where there is only love.

You've never seen me crying, have you – Angela?
Come closer so you can taste the salt – Angela –
I will name each tear and let it run like a river
into the sea, the sea, the sea. I'll use the knife blade –
Angela – to carve tributaries from my eyes.
There is no evidence in support of love.

I will etch my face into a window of stained glass.

I will etch my face into a cathedral of disappointment.

How often – Angela – does life give us

the opportunity to do the right thing? O –

Angela – O –

Every day –

Every day –

Every day.

www.ingramcontent.com/pod-product-compliance
Ingram Content Group UK Ltd.
Pitfield, Milton Keynes, MK11 3LW, UK
UKHW062308290726
14090UKWH00018B/940